# BIG
## Nature
## Facts

**BIG NATURE FACTS PHOTOGRAPHIC CREDITS**

p6 Manfred Danegger NHPA; p7 Laurie Campbell NHPA; p9 bl Stephen Meyers Ardea, tr Manfred Danegger NHPA, p13 b John Daniels Ardea: p15 t Robert Maier Bruce Coleman Collection , b Pictor International, p16-17 b Laurie Campbell NHPA; 17 t Gerard Laez FLPA; p18 b Joe Blossom NHPA; p19 t George McCarthy Bruce Coleman Collection; b Martin Withers FLPA; p 20 tr Neil McIntyre Getty Images; p24 Jane Burton Warren Photographic; p26 t Susane Danegger NHPA; p27 b Jane Burton Warren Photographic; p30 tl Jean Louis Le Moigne NHPA; p31 tr Hugh Clark FLPA; p33 tl Richard Packwood Oxford Scientific Films, tr Mark Hamblin Oxford Scientific Films, bl M J Thomas FLPA, c Yann Arthus-Bertrand Ardea, p35 t Stephen Dalton NHPA; p36 bl Hellio & Van Ingen NHPA, br Gordon Langsbury Bruce Coleman Collection, t E Woods FLPA; 37 t Michael Leach NHPA, b G I Bernard Oxford Scientific Films; 38 & 39 Jane Burton Warren Photographic; 42 b Manfred Danegger NHPA, t David Thomson Oxford Scientific Films; 46 bl Peter Cade Getty Images, tr Terry Heathcote Oxford Scientific Films; 47 Heather Angel Natural Visions; 50 cl Geoff Bryant NHPA, bl Heather Angel; 51 bl H Clark FLPA, cr Kenneth W Fink Ardea; 54 b Manfred Danegger NHPA, t A P Barnes NHPA; 57 bl Anthea Sieveking Collections, tr John R Bracegirdle, 58 Stephen Dalton NHPA, 59 tl Walter Murray NHPA, tc & tr Jane Burton Warren Photographic; 64 tr Heather Angel Natural Visions; 65 tc Martin Garwood NHPA tr Stephen Dalton NHPA; 66 bl Heather Angel Natural Visions; 69 Roger Jackman Oxford Scientific Films, br Jane Burton Warren Photographic; 70 bl Ian West Bubbles, t David Fox Oxford Scientific Films; 71 FLPA/Foto Natura J Van Arkel; 72 bl Tony & Liz Bomford Ardea, tr Francois Gohier Ardea, 73 r Andy Rouse, 76 bl Vince Streano Corbis, br & 76/77 Francois Gohier Ardea; 78 b Heather Angel Natural Visions, t Ron Austing FLPA; 79 t Pictor International, br Heather Angel Natural Visions;

This paperback edition published in 2005 by Armadillo Books
An imprint of Bookmart Limited
Registered Number 2372865
Trading as Bookmart Limited
Blaby Road, Wigston
Leicestershire, LE18 4SE, UK

10 9 8 7 6 5 4 3 2 1

© 2002 Bookmart Limited

ISBN 1-84322-426-7

Printed in Singapore

# BIG
# Nature
# Facts

# Contents

# Foxes

## At home with foxes

A fox's home is called an "earth". This may be a hole which the fox digs or a burrow left by a badger or some other animal.

## Look out for...

A fox's footprint is five to six centimetres long. A fox leaves a long, thin line of footprints, which are called "tracks".

## Family life

The female fox is called a "vixen". The male fox is a "dog". The vixen has four or five babies or "cubs".

Foxes are "nocturnal" which means they rest in the day and come out at night to look for food.

# Squirrels

## Squirrel cousins

Once red squirrels were very common, then grey squirrels took over the woods and drove them out. Now red squirrels are quite rare in many countries.

### Cosy homes

Squirrels live in trees. Look for their nests, or "dreys", made from leaves, twigs and grass.

# Rabbits

## Watch out!

Rabbits have large eyes and long ears. They are always looking and listening for danger as they nibble the grass or dig their burrows. They stamp their feet to warn each other of danger.

## Rabbit prints

See if you can spot rabbit footprints in soft earth. Their front feet make small, round prints and their back feet make long prints.

# Hares

## All about hares

Hares may be grey or brown: you are most likely to see a brown hare. It lives mainly on farmland.

Male hares are called "jacks" and females are called "does".

## Mad March hares

In early spring, hares seem to go mad. The males chase each other and females fight off the males by boxing them!

Hares have long legs, so they can run away from hunters at top speed. They can run as fast as the best racehorses!

### Look out for...

Hares look like big rabbits but they are almost twice as big and have much longer ears and legs.

Rabbit      Hare

# Meadows

## What is a meadow?

A meadow is a field of grass that is cut once a year to make hay for cows to eat in winter.

Farmers make hay at the end of the summer. For the rest of the year the meadow is home to all kinds of animals and flowers.

Ragged robin got its name because of its long, thin petals, which make its flowers look ragged.

Busy bumble-bees buzz around meadows on warm days looking for flowers.

The ox-eye daisy has large petals and yellow centres which are easy for insects to land on.

The harvestman looks like a long-legged spider. It hunts small insects in the grass.

Brown hares dig a dip or "form" in the soil to hide in.

The common blue butterfly is often seen in meadows. Its caterpillars feed on clover.

Poppies have oval seed pods which sprinkle seeds as the wind shakes them.

Fritillaries are bell-shaped flowers which are usually purple.

Partridges hide in meadows searching for insects to eat.

Field voles come out of their underground holes to nibble at grass roots.

Most clover stalks have three leaves but look out for four, they're lucky!

11

# Sheep

### Lamby families!

Sheep are farm animals. They eat grass and can live anywhere grassy – even on hills.

Male sheep are called "rams". They have horns to fight with. Female sheep are "ewes" and their babies are called "lambs".

### All about wool

Sheep are covered in woolly fur, called a "fleece". The farmer cuts off or "shears" the fleece to make into wool. This doesn't hurt – it's like having a haircut!

### Woolly clothes

The fleeces from the sheep are cleaned and brushed. Then strands are wound together to make long strings of wool to knit into hats, gloves, scarves and jumpers.

# Pigs

## Pretty pigs

Saddleback pigs are a special type of pig. They have a white patch on their backs that looks like a saddle.

## All about pigs

They snort, squeal, grunt and go "Oink". The most common are pink, but some are black and white or spotted. They walk on their "trotters" and they eat almost anything.

## Family life

Pigs live on farms. They have round noses called "snouts", big ears and curly, twitchy tails.

Male pigs are called "boars" and females are known as "sows". Baby pigs are called "piglets". Pigs have big families. A sow can have as many as 15 piglets at a time!

# Horses

## Fun with foals

Baby horses are called "foals". They have long, thin legs and can walk almost as soon as they are born. A foal stays near to its mother because it feeds on her milk.

## Little ponies

Shetland ponies are tiny! They only grow up to 1.2 metres or 40 inches tall – that's about the same size as a six-year-old child.

They are often city farm pets as they are gentle and they like children.

## What are donkeys?

Donkeys are just like little horses. The main differences are that they have bigger ears, longer coats and shorter, fatter tails.

Male donkeys are called "jacks", females are "mares" and babies are "foals", just like horses.

There is also an animal called a "mule", which is half donkey and half horse!

# Cows

## All about cows

Cows are farm animals. They eat grass to make the milk we drink and pour on to our breakfast cereal.

The farmer milks his dairy cows twice a day. He brings them in from the fields in the morning and again in the afternoon.

## Happy families

Male cows are called "bulls", females are called "cows" and the babies are "calves". Bulls have big horns and can be very dangerous.

Cows have calves in the spring when there is lots of new grass for the mothers to eat to make them strong.

**Highland cattle**

## Cow colours

There are many different types of cow. You may have seen black and white cows called "Friesians". Most of the milk we drink comes from Friesian cows.

Jersey cows are a golden brown colour. They give rich, creamy milk.

**Jersey cows**
The creamy milk from these lovely Jersey cows is used to make toffee and fudge. Yum!

**Friesian cows**
These are the most popular cows for milk or dairy herds. See if you can count how many are in the fields near you.

17

# Goats

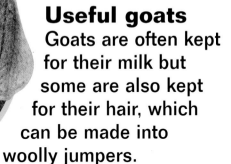

### Goat families

Male and female goats have special names. Males are called "billy" goats and females are called "nanny" goats. Babies are called "kids".

### Useful goats

Goats are often kept for their milk but some are also kept for their hair, which can be made into woolly jumpers.

### Playful goats

Pet goats like to be stroked and are very playful creatures. They will eat almost anything, including clothes and sweets!

# Badgers

## Home sweet home

Badgers live below ground in a big burrow called a "sett". There are lots of entrances and many rooms, linked together by tunnels.

Two badger families will often share a sett, using different chambers for having babies and for sleeping.

## Badger babies

Baby badgers are born in a warm nest, deep down in the sett. They stay here until they are eight weeks old. After this they are big enough to come out and play in the woods in the evenings.

19

# Deer

## Amazing antlers

Female deer and their babies are gentle-looking creatures with big eyes, but the male deer (the "stag") is much larger and grows huge antlers. The male's antlers grow for the first time when the stag is a year old. Every winter, the antlers drop off, but each spring the male grows a new, bigger set.

## Mummy deer

Mother deer are always alert to danger. Their sensitive ears and nose twitch as they keep a lookout for enemies while their calves graze in safety.

## There's deer about!
Even though deer are shy, they leave many signs behind – if you know what to look for. Watch out for deer footprints, which are called "slots". See if you can spot damaged bark on trees. This is where stags rub their antlers against tree trunks.

## Spotted babies
Female red deer are called "hinds". Each year they have a baby called a "calf". The males are called "stags".

Red deer calves are covered with white spots to make it harder for other animals to see them.

## Hide!
A mother will leave very young babies hidden in long grass while she goes to eat.

# Caves

## It's dark in there!

Caves are formed by underground rivers or by waves wearing into the rock. Caves make safe homes for many animals, especially "nocturnal" or night-time ones.

House martins make cone-shaped mud nests in cave entrances.

The Greater Horseshoe bat gets its name from its horseshoe-shaped nose.

This is a spitting spider. It traps insects to eat by spitting sticky threads over them.

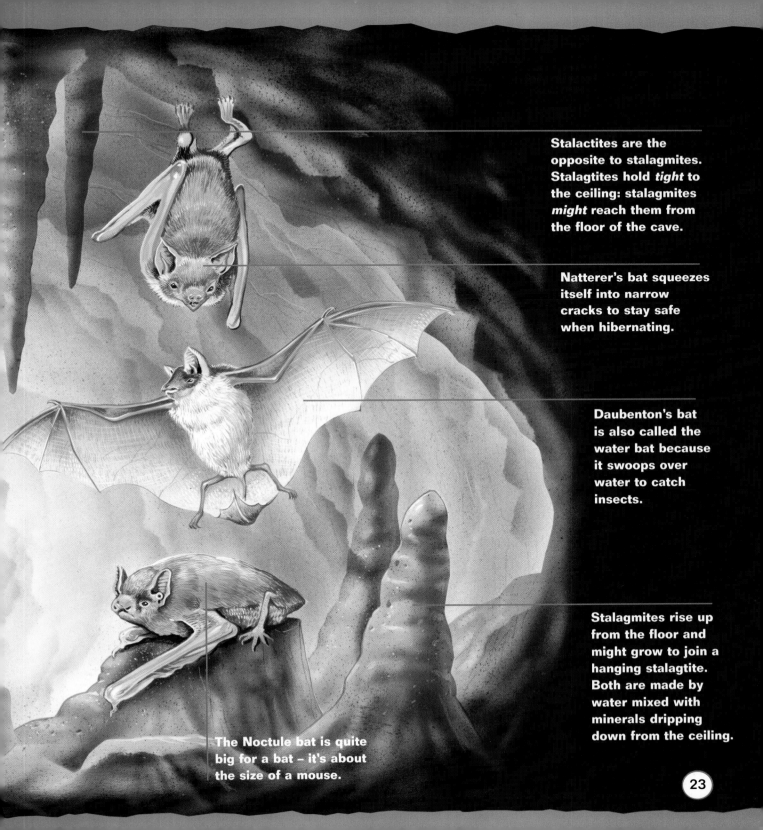

Stalactites are the opposite to stalagmites. Stalagtites hold *tight* to the ceiling: stalagmites *might* reach them from the floor of the cave.

Natterer's bat squeezes itself into narrow cracks to stay safe when hibernating.

Daubenton's bat is also called the water bat because it swoops over water to catch insects.

Stalagmites rise up from the floor and might grow to join a hanging stalagtite. Both are made by water mixed with minerals dripping down from the ceiling.

The Noctule bat is quite big for a bat – it's about the size of a mouse.

# Ducks

## What's inside?

Inside every egg there's a tiny speck a bit like a seed. This is the bit that will grow into a duck. The egg yolk is food for the baby to eat as it grows.

This baby Aylesbury duck is ready to hatch.

The duckling pecks a hole in the shell with its beak.

Then it pushes against the shell and wriggles out.

It rests again before kicking off the shell.

Free at last!

Two days later, the duckling is ready for its first swim!

## In a flap!

Ducks stay dry even when they are paddling on ponds because their feathers are covered in waterproof oils. The layers of feathers trap air beneath them. This helps them to float and keeps them warm, just like a duvet. Sometimes they flap their wings to dry them, and sometimes just for fun!

## Duck-dive

A duck upends itself to feed: it sticks its head underwater and paddles its webbed feet to keep its head under water as it feeds on pondweed and snails.

25

# Geese

## Feathered friends

Geese are useful to farmers, as they eat grass and provide eggs and soft feathers for pillows.

They make good burglar alarms too, hissing or honking loudly at strangers or intruders like foxes (left).

## Feathered families

Geese belong to the same "family" as ducks and swans called "waterfowl". They all have broad, boat-shaped bodies, strong legs and large, webbed feet which make them very good swimmers. But when they are on land it also makes them walk awkwardly – they waddle! And when a goose "talks' it is said to be gobbling.

# Chicks and hens

## Chickens galore!

Baby chickens are called "chicks" and their mothers are called "hens". Hens and chicks live on farms all over the world. In fact, there are more chickens on Earth than people!

When chicks hatch out from their eggs, they can walk and feed themselves straight away. As the hen scrapes the ground with her feet, they peck at any seeds she digs up.

## Cockerels

Male chickens are called "cockerels". They have big red crests on top of their heads and red "wattles" hanging under their chins.

# Seabirds

## Who lives on cliffs?

Lots of seabirds make their nests and lay their eggs on cliffs, especially in spring and summer. Cliffs are good places for birds to bring up chicks because hunters such as foxes cannot get to them. All these birds can make cliff tops interesting – but very noisy!

The fulmar looks a bit like a seagull. If its nest is disturbed, the fulmar squirts out nasty smelling liquid from its beak.

Gannets are one of the biggest seabirds. To catch fish, they dive into the water from the air.

The chough (say "chuff") is a type of crow with a red, curving beak and red legs. The chough flies like an acrobat as it rolls in the wind.

The shag has a long pointed beak which it uses to catch fish. In cloudy weather, its feathers look black, but in bright sunlight, you can see that they are shiny and dark green.

Razorbills like to live together in huge groups. To find food, they swim on the sea like ducks, then dive underwater to catch fish.

The rock dove looks just like a town pigeon. It lives on cliffs all year round, but usually flies inland to find food.

Puffins are easy to spot. They have white faces, clown-like eyes, big, stripy beaks and orange legs. Puffins make their nests in burrows at the top of cliffs.

# Nesting birds

## Hidden nests!

It's not easy to spot wild creatures' nests. Birds keep their nests out of reach and well hidden to protect their eggs and chicks.

## Look up!

Birds nest in buildings, caves, hedges, cliffs and (of course) in trees. Small birds, like finches, hide away for safety. But large birds, like crows, make big, untidy nests that can be seen from the ground.

## Special nests

Swallows and house martens build cup-shaped nests of mud in the corners of farm buildings, where the wall meets the roof. See if you can spot one!

## Garden nests

Even garden birds build nests. They make them from twigs, moss, grass and feathers. Encourage birds into your garden with a bird box like this one. You may be lucky: a bird might choose yours for their eggs to hatch into 'fledglings'.

# Garden birds

## Naughty nuts

Attract birds into your garden by leaving tasty titbits where only they can reach. Peanuts are good for garden birds in winter, but not when they're feeding their chicks in summer. A baby bird could choke on a big peanut.

## Bird feeders

Scatter breadcrumbs, raisins and seeds on a feeder or window sill to attract birds to your garden.

## Garden furniture

Bird boxes, bird tables and garden furniture make ideal feeding sites. If you stock up every day, the birds will soon visit to look for food. Experiment with different sorts of food. Try bacon rinds, or seeds, as well as breadcrumbs and crusts.

## Windblown

Stormy winds often blow nests away – you may find them in your garden.

## Bugs for breakfast

In summer, birds like wrens and flycatchers look for insects to feed to their babies. Ponds and plants will attract insects into your garden and the birds will soon come after them!

**Wren**

**Flycatchers**

## We love weeds!

To attract birds to your garden, it shouldn't be too tidy. Let a patch of weeds, such as nettles, dandelions and thistles, grow. Or grow sunflowers. These will make seeds for the birds to eat.

# Owls

## What are owls?

Owls are meat-eating birds. They hunt mostly at night for mice and other small animals. They have sharp claws for catching them and hooked beaks for eating them.

## Barn owls

The beautiful barn owl makes its nest in old barns. This night-time hunter is also known as the screech owl because of its high-pitched, screeching call.

# Bats

## All about bats

Bats are small, furry mammals with wings.

As bats fly, they make high-pitched sounds, which we cannot hear. They listen for the echo from this sound and use it to find moths and other food.

## Bats bedtime

Many bats use barns as places to sleep during the day, coming out at night. Others go to sleep for the entire winter. This is called "hibernating".

# Kestrels

## Floating on air

The kestrel is a bird of prey. This means that it is a skilled hunter. It can float in the air in one place, even when there's no wind. This is called "hovering". As it hovers, the kestrel looks for small animals to eat on the ground below.

## Baby-sitting

Kestrels lay their eggs in spring. The mother lays four or five eggs. Then she sits on them for a month until they hatch, while the male kestrel brings her food.

## Kestrel-spotting

If you see a bird of prey with pointed wings, hovering, it's probably a kestrel. If it has rounded wings and is flying fast and low, it's a sparrowhawk.

## Flying high

Birds of prey have grown accustomed to town life. The kestrel is one of many birds of prey you may spot flying high in the sky over towns and cities, as well as in the countryside. Watch them hover, then swoop.

## Motorway kestrels

Look out for kestrels on motorway journeys. They often hover over the sides of roads, looking for small animals, like voles or mice, in the grass verges below.

# Cats

## The friendly hunter

Cats and humans have lived together for thousands of years because cats make excellent pets. But cats still have a wild side. They are clever hunters and will catch small animals even when they're well-fed.

## Playful kittens

Kittens love to play with each other and often have pretend fights. Playing helps them to learn to hunt.

## Nine lives

Cats are so good at getting out of sticky situations that people often say they have nine lives. In fact, they are very agile and good at slipping their way out of danger. They have keen eyesight and their whiskers help them to sense things.

# Dogs

## Knowing noses

Dogs love humans and make great pets, but they are also useful for other reasons. They have an excellent sense of smell and can use their noses to sniff out all sorts of things. Police sniffer dogs are trained to follow a person's trail and find hidden objects.

## Playtime

Puppies love playing. They love to run, chase and fetch, and some dogs are trained to do all these things. When your puppy crouches on its front legs with its bottom in the air and wags it tail, it wants to play.

## Puppy fun

If you leave your puppy on its own, give it a toy to play with so that it does not chew the furniture!

# Life underground

## A safe place

It is warm and dark under the ground. Some animals hide here in winter to escape the cold – and some never come out at all!

In winter, rabbits spend a lot of time in their burrows underground.

Toads use natural holes, or other animals' burrows, to escape the cold. They come out in spring.

Roots help plants to take in water. They also fix plants in the soil to stop them being blown over.

The centipede lives in the soil, where it hunts tiny animals. It has more than 100 legs.

Leatherjackets are young insects that eat roots. They come above ground in summer and turn into daddy-long-legs, which are also known as crane-flies.

Blackbirds use their sharp beaks to search for worms and insects in the ground.

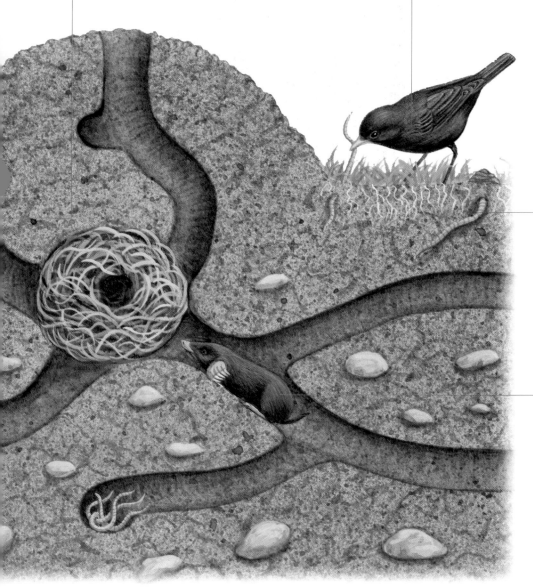

Earthworms eat as they go along and leave piles or "casts" of earth behind them.

Tiny adult moles make grass nests in the ground for their babies. They store food, such as worms, in tunnels just like in a larder or pantry!

# Moles

## Little digger

Moles are small furry mammals that live underground in tunnels.

They have big front paws to help them dig. If a mole is above ground, it can dig its way out of sight in just 15 seconds!

## Babies

Baby moles are born with no hair and they cannot move. Their mother feeds them until they leave the nest at five weeks old. Then they start looking for food on their own.

Moles have whiskers on their noses to help them feel their way around.

Moles can close up their ears so that no dirt gets into them.

A mole's hair is soft and sticks upwards. It never tangles and helps the mole move easily in tunnels.

Moles are about the length of an adult's hand but their front paws are very big.

Fine hairs on the mole's tail help it to feel food or danger behind it.

# Feeling their way

Moles feel their way around in the dark using their sensitive noses and tails.

They cannot see or hear very well, but their sense of smell is excellent.

## Molehills

You can tell where a mole has been by looking for molehills. These raised piles of soil are made by a mole as it digs through the earth.

# How plants grow

## Bright and beautiful

Plants use sunlight to make the food that they need to grow. They also need water and a gas from the air.

Leaves are green because of a chemical in them that uses light to make food for the plant.

## Water for life

Plants need water to live. Their roots suck the water up out of the soil, along with other good nutrients. That is why we water the soil that plants grow in.

If a plant sucks up too much water, it releases the extra back into the air through its leaves.

# Full of beans

When a seed starts to grow it is often buried deep under the ground. So how does it know which way to grow? Try this easy bean experiment to find out!

**3** In the next few days, you will see shoots appear. Which way are they growing? Put the jar on a sunny window sill and watch how quickly the shoots grow.

**2** Put the jar in a dark place and check the beans each day. In a few days you will see them start to sprout roots. Which way are the roots growing?

**1** Fit a piece of blotting paper into a jar and add 2cm (1 inch) of water. Put six dried beans (pinto or kidney) between the paper and the side of the jar.

## How do beans do it?

Even when a seed is in total darkness and upside down, the roots grow downwards. Gravity, the invisible force, pulls everything downwards into the ground. Shoots grow up towards the light because sunlight makes their food.

45

# Trees

### Types of tree

Like other plants, trees grow by taking up water through their roots. They also use sunlight to make food in their leaves.

Some trees keep their leaves all year. These are called "evergreens". Some lose their leaves in winter. These are called "deciduous".

### Falling leaves

In autumn when there is less sun and the ground begins to freeze, deciduous trees lose their leaves. The tree then rests for the winter.

## Signs of life

In winter many trees have no leaves. But look closely and you will see buds on the twigs. Inside each bud there are tiny leaves which will grow in the spring.

## Open up

As it gets warmer, the bud gets fatter. A new shoot begins to push its way out. It has new leaves curled around it.

## Catkins

Many trees, like the silver birch, have dangly catkins in the spring. These are its flowers.

The catkins hang down to make it easier for the wind to blow the pollen away to fertilise other silver birches.

## Last year's scars

Look for ring marks on a tree branch. These are where the buds from previous years grew. The rings are called "girdle scars".

# Leaves

## Let's look at leaves

Take a look at a leaf. Some trees, such as beech, oak, plane and chestnut, have flat leaves which fan out to catch the sun.

Turn your leaf over. The back of the leaf has veins to carry food and water between the leaf and the tree.

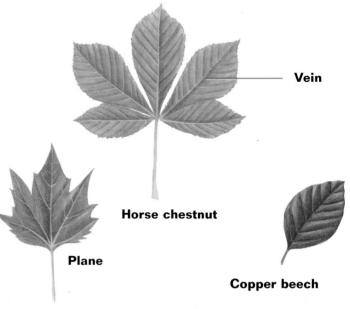

Vein

Horse chestnut

Oak

Plane

Copper beech

## Autumn leaves

Before they fall off, leaves turn brown as the chemical which makes them green is sucked back into the tree.

## Evergreen leaves

Evergreens, like pine trees, have narrow leaves, called "needles". These are tough and do not dry up, so they make some food for the tree even in winter.

New needles grow all year as the old ones fall, so evergreens are always covered in needles.

## Weather forecast

Evergreen trees store their seeds inside a cone. When it rains, the cone stays shut. When the weather is warm and dry, the scales of the cone open up and the breeze carries the seeds away.

49

# Flowers

## Surviving the cold

Snowdrops and crocuses have bulbs at the bottom of their stems, where food is stored during the chilly winter months.

When the days get warmer, the plants use the energy from this food to push their stems up through the soil and to grow flowers.

**Snowdrop**

## Tough life

Buddleia is a garden plant that now grows wild in many towns. It is very tough and can grow where most plants can not.

Buddleia is also called the "butterfly plant" as butterflies love feeding on its nectar.

## Deadly blooms

Foxgloves look very pretty but they are dangerous to eat! Even though they are deadly, they can save lives. Scientists use chemicals in foxgloves to make medicine for people with bad hearts.

## Bucket plant

The tank bromeliad is a tropical plant which has special leaves. The leaves can catch and store as much water as six watering cans for the plant.

# Hedgerow life

## Hedge roads

Hedgerows make perfect homes for animals and plants because they offer shelter and food.

They also link up so that animals can run from place to place.

**Tiny wrens perch in hedgerows looking for tasty insects and berries to eat.**

**Spiders make their webs in hedgerows where there are lots of insects for them to catch in their webs.**

**Birds eat rosehips and drop the seeds. These grow into dog roses.**

**The slow worm looks like a snake but it is actually a lizard with no legs. Slow worms often live in hedgerows and feed on slugs.**

The prickly holly bush has white summer flowers and bright red berries in the autumn.

The dunnock is also known as the hedgerow sparrow. It builds its nest and hunts for food in the hedgerow.

Honeysuckle stems twist through the hedgerows. The flowers attract butterflies and bees.

Wild primroses often grow in the sheltered banks at the bottom of hedgerows.

The common dormouse usually lives in woodlands but it often travels through hedgerows. Some dormice enjoy hedgerow life so much, they move in for good!

# Hedgehogs

## Spiky friends

Hedgehogs are small, wild, spiky animals that live under hedgerows and eat insects. If they are in danger, they can curl up into a tight ball and their spikes protect them.

### Nests

Hedgehogs make warm nests in the autumn. They also eat lots. Then they curl up to sleep, or "hibernate", right through the cold winter months.

## Follow the leader

When they are three weeks old, baby hedgehogs come out of their nest and follow their mother – often in a single line. They learn how to search for food and what to do if they are in danger.

# Dormice

## On the look-out

The dormouse has big eyes and long, sensitive whiskers to help it to find food in the dark.

It has good hearing too. It listens out for night-time hunters who may be looking for a small, mousy meal!

## Look out for...

Dormice eat nuts by gnawing a hole in the shell to get at the food inside.

Nuts eaten by a dormouse have scratchy toothmarks on the shell around a hole.

# Insects

## Looking at insects

All sorts of strange creatures live among the grass. Try trapping some to take a look.

### Building your trap

Dig a hole in the soil and put a clean yoghurt pot or jam jar in it. Make sure the rim is level with the surface. Put a piece of apple inside. Put two pebbles on either side of the trap and rest a flat stone on top to protect it from rain and sun.

## Taking a closer look

Keep checking and you will see some visitors to your pot. Use a magnifying glass to take a look at them.

When you have finished, remember to set the insects free in the same place as they were caught.

# Bees

## Where is honey from?
We all know that honey comes from bees, but how do they actually make it? In a factory or a kitchen? No! Clever little bees make honey in their tummies!

## Busy bees
Worker bees collect pollen from flowers to feed the other bees in the hive. Can you see this bee's pollen sacks on its legs?

## How is honey made?
Bees collect nectar from flowers with their tongues. In the bee's tummy, the nectar mixes with special chemicals and turns into honey. Back at the bee's home or "hive", it stores the honey in holes called "cells" in a "honeycomb". Bee keepers collect the honey from the hives.

# Butterflies

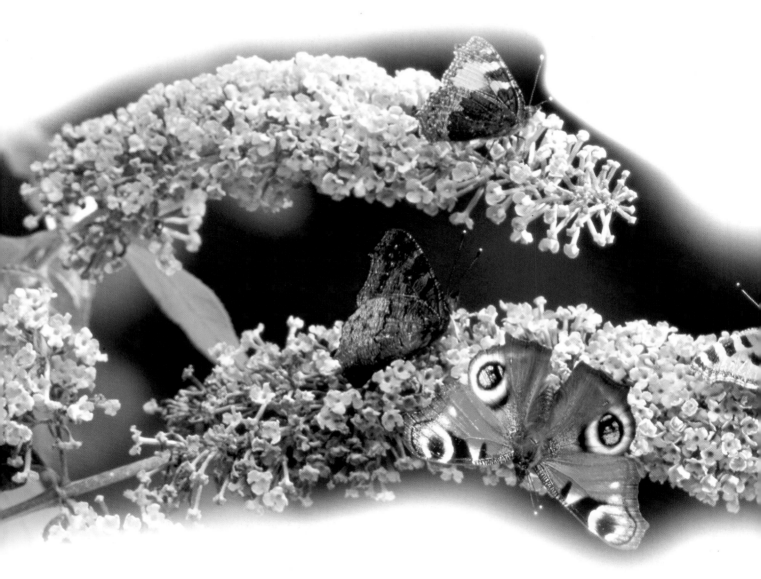

### Scary eyes!
Butterflies' wings are covered with tiny, colourful scales. Some have patterns that look like the eyes of larger animals. This helps them to fool hunters.

## A butterfly is born
Here is how a little egg becomes a lovely butterfly…

Butterflies lay lots of tiny eggs. Most lay them on the leaves of plants that their caterpillars like to eat.

The eggs hatch out into tiny caterpillars after a few weeks. The caterpillars eat leaves to grow big and fat.

When they are big enough, they spin a coat of silky threads around themselves. This silky coat is called a "chrysalis".

Slowly, the caterpillar inside the chrysalis changes into a butterfly. After a few weeks, the new butterfly breaks out and flies away!

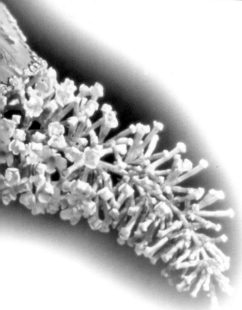

## Where to see butterflies
You can see lots of different butterflies in the summer, feeding on the sweet nectar of flowers. Butterflies have their favourite plants. One is the butterfly bush (its proper name is "buddleia": see page 51). Look for this plant, covered in butterflies, in your garden or in the park.

# On the seabed

A squid is a bit like an octopus, but it has big eyes and ten tentacles (long arms) instead of eight.

## In the darkness
Most deep sea animals are fish. You might have heard of some of them, like cod, haddock and plaice, as they are served up in fish restaurants all around the world. These fish share their home with spider crabs, anglerfish and squid.

It's dark down on the seabed so creatures that live there need to see well to find food and spot the animals that might eat them.

The anglerfish is scary-looking. It moves the long bony bit over its nose backwards and forwards, like a fishing rod, to catch fish.

The spider crab has long legs to help it walk quickly over the sea bottom. Its tough, spiky shell protects it from big fish that might want to eat it.

Cod are big fish that travel in groups called "shoals". They can grow up to 1.5 metres long, which is the height of a 14 year old girl!

The conger eel is a big, long fish. It prefers to live among rocks or ship wrecks where it can hide and then dart out to grab its prey.

Lobsters are related to crabs and shrimps. They use their big "pincers" or claws to collect food and protect themselves.

The plaice is flat like a plate. Its eyes are on the top of its head. When it hides under the sand only its eyes poke out. This is how it watches out for danger.

# Minibeasts

## Mini world of wonders

There is a tiny world of wildlife to explore on every patch of earth. There are hundreds of different minibeasts living on or under the ground. All you need to do is kneel down and take a look!

The common toad looks like a frog but it has drier skin and walks rather than hops.

This burrowing centipede is often found in gardens. "Centipede" means "one hundred feet" but most have fewer.

Ants live together in big nests underground. One nest can have thousands of ants in it!

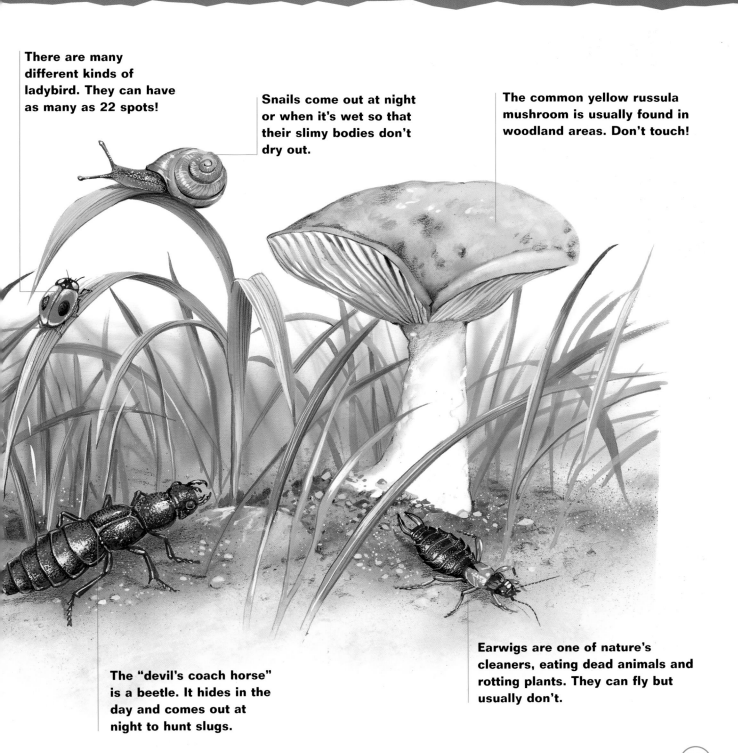

There are many different kinds of ladybird. They can have as many as 22 spots!

Snails come out at night or when it's wet so that their slimy bodies don't dry out.

The common yellow russula mushroom is usually found in woodland areas. Don't touch!

The "devil's coach horse" is a beetle. It hides in the day and comes out at night to hunt slugs.

Earwigs are one of nature's cleaners, eating dead animals and rotting plants. They can fly but usually don't.

# Spiders

## Super spiders

Spiders are interesting creatures. Many people think that spiders are insects, but all insects have six legs. Spiders have eight, and are called "arachnids". Many have eight eyes too.

Look closely at spiders' webs. The patterns they weave are amazing.

**Wolf spider**

## Tarantulas

Wild tarantulas live in rainforests. Tarantulas are shy spiders and like to hide but tame ones will come out for a walk – across your hand!

## What's for tea?

Most spiders eat insects. The wolf spider chases insects. Others, such as the jumping spider, lie in wait, then leap on them. But most catch insects in their webs.

Many people are frightened of spiders but those in your home or garden are harmless.

# Ladybirds

## What are ladybirds?

Ladybirds are a type of flying beetle. They can be red, orange, yellow or black in colour.

Ladybirds eat greenflies which can damage plants. Gardeners love ladybirds because they stop greenflies eating their plants.

## Dotty bugs

Red ladybirds with seven spots are the ones you are most likely to see.

## Sweet dreams!

In autumn, ladybirds gather in large groups to "hibernate" or sleep through the winter.

# Frogs

## The life of a frog

Frogs and toads are "amphibians" which means that they can live both on land and in water.

They eat insects by catching them on the end of their long, sticky tongues.

## I can see you

Frogs eyes are on top of their heads. This means they can lay underwater and look up without being seen.

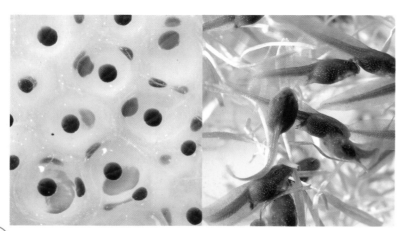

## Froggy families

In spring, frogs lay their eggs, which are called "frogspawn", in water.

"Tadpoles" or baby frogs hatch out from these eggs. As the weeks pass, tadpoles grow legs and lose their tails. Then they become little frogs.

# Snakes

## S-s-s-snakes!

Snakes are strange creatures. They have no legs or eyelids and can be as small as a pencil or as long as a lorry!

They eat meat, from snails to goats, depending on their size, killing them with a poison bite or by strangling.

## Sniffing snakes

Snakes can't hear very well, but they have a strong sense of smell.

A snake smells by sticking out its tongue and collecting smells from the air. Cells in its mouth send messages to the brain, which works out what is nearby.

## Slithery moves

Snakes move by coiling and uncoiling themselves. They push with one part and pull with another.

## Skinny skin skin

Snakes' scales are covered by a thin skin. Snakes shed their skin every year. They wriggle out of them, leaving them on the ground like a rolled-up sock.

# Life on the river bed

## Glorious mud

As rivers flow, they wash away soil and sand from the banks. These mix with rotting leaves and dead insects in the water, turning into thick mud which sinks to the river bed. Lots of river animals love to live here, where it's warm, dark and safe.

### Spotting willows

Have you seen a beautiful weeping willow tree beside a pond or river? Look for its long, drooping branches hanging down and often trailing in the water. Willow twigs are bendy so people use them to make baskets or chairs.

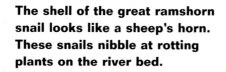

The shell of the great ramshorn snail looks like a sheep's horn. These snails nibble at rotting plants on the river bed.

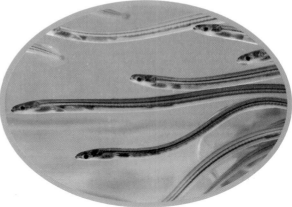

Eels are long, thin fish with two tiny fins. They lie in the mud on the river bed, catching smaller fish and insects to eat.

Frogs spend the winter buried in the mud at the bottom of rivers and ponds.

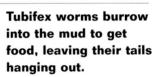

Tubifex worms burrow into the mud to get food, leaving their tails hanging out.

# Snappy crabs

## All about crabs

Crabs have hard shells all over their bodies and big pincers. They have eight legs and walk sideways because of the way that their legs join together. If they didn't scamper sideways, their legs would get tangled up with each other!

## At the seaside

Many different types of crab live at the seashore. The one that people see most often is the shore crab. You may spot one on the rocks or scuttling across the seaweed!

## Empty shells

You may find empty crab shells next time you go to the beach. Don't worry, they're not dead crabs, they're just old crab shells. Most crabs' shells come off every few months, as the crab inside grows bigger.

## Hermit crabs

Hermit crabs often use the empty shells of shellfish, such as periwinkles and whelks, for added protection.

# Seals

## What are seals?

Seals are large animals that live in the sea. They are mammals like we are, so they breathe air. But they can dive underwater and stay there for a long time, using their flippers to swim fast.

Most seals are about as long as an adult and some males are much longer!

## Super swimmers

Seals chase and catch fish to eat. They hunt for them underwater off coasts and around islands.

Their bodies are perfect for swimming. Seals swim with their tails, which end in two big flippers. They steer with two smaller flippers that stick out like arms.

## Nosy seals

Seals are nosy animals. They often pop their heads above the water to have a look at boats. Sailors used to think that they were mermaids!

# Rock pools

## What are rock pools?

A rock pool is a shallow hole in the rocks on the beach which is full of seawater. Most rock pools are refilled twice a day when the tide comes in.

You can find rock pools on most beaches. They are good places to discover creatures such as crabs, mussels and barnacles.

### Sharp shells

Be careful around rock pools! The water may not be very deep but the seaweed around them can be very slippery and some of the shells are sharp.

Barnacles are tiny shellfish that cling to the rocks. Their shells are sharp and can cut your feet.

Bladderwrack has air bags in its fronds. When this seaweed is underwater, the air bags lift the fronds towards the light.

The blenny is a fish that uses the fins under its chin like legs to hold itself up off the rock when resting!

You will often see sea lettuce in rock pools. It gets its name because it looks like salad lettuce!

The oystercatcher is easy to spot because it has bold black and white feathers and a very long, orange beak.

If you see a crab at the beach, it is most likely to be a shore crab.

Limpets move very slowly, feeding on tiny plants called "algae" that grow on the rocks.

The sea anemone catches small animals to eat in its tentacles.

The spiny starfish isn't actually a fish! It is a boneless animal that is shaped like a star with five arms.

# Dolphins

## Dolphin families

Most dolphins like to be with other dolphins. They move around together in groups called "pods". They are very clever animals and have many ways of "talking" to each other.

Dolphins often leap out of the wat and into the air. Some people think they do this to breathe or as a sig to other dolphins, others think the do it for fun.

## Spot the difference

Dolphins and their cousins the porpoises are about the same size and shape. To tell them apart, look at their noses.

Dolphins have a nose shaped like a peaked cap. Porpoises have a rounder nose, with no bulge, as shown in the picture of the girl and the porpoise.

## Finding food

Dolphins can see underwater but they find food by using sound. As they swim, they make clicks and squeaks. The sounds travel through the sea until they hit something solid, like a fish. The sound bounces back as an echo so the dolphins can work out where the fish is.

As it leaps, a dolphin breathes in air through a hole at the top of its head.

Some dolphins have a curvy mouth that makes them look as if they're smiling.

# Animals in danger

### Tiger alert

All tigers are "endangered" which means that there are only a few left in the wild.

The Javan tiger died out or "became extinct" in 1979 and the Indo-Chinese tiger (right) may soon die out too. There are just eighty left in the wild.

### Homeless pandas

The panda's home in the bamboo forests of China is being cut down. Only one thousand pandas are now left in the wild.

# BIG
# Nature
# Facts

## Happy story

Otters almost disappeared from Britain just 50 years ago.

Since then, many dirty rivers have been cleaned and otter hunting is banned. Otters are now coming back to Britain.

## The last of the elephants

African elephants are hunted for their valuable ivory tusks. Asian elephants are in danger because their forest home is being destroyed.

## Rare orchid

Plants can also become endangered. Some beautiful flowers, such as the ghost orchid, are very rare today.